Hunger is the best sauce.

Country Living

Notes *from*
a Country
Cupboard

Page 84: Excerpt from "Serve It Forth," in *The Art of Eating*, by
M.F.K. Fisher, 1976. Copyright © 1990 by M.F.K. Fisher. Reprinted with
permission of Macmillan Publishing Company.

Additional credits and acknowledgments appear on page 96.

ISBN: 0-688-13408-4

Printed in Singapore
First Edition
1 2 3 4 5 6 7 8 9 10

Country Living Staff
Rachel Newman, Editor-in-Chief
Niña Williams, Executive Editor
Julio Vega, Art Director
Mary R. Roby, Managing Editor
Joanne Lamb Hayes, Food Editor
John Mack Carter, Director, Magazine Development

Produced by Smallwood and Stewart, Inc., New York City

Edited by Rachel Carley
Designed by Jan Melchior

Contents

Introduction

I don't do as much cooking these days as I'd like to, but I haven't forgotten the pleasure of preparing food for friends and family, and I certainly haven't forgotten the kitchen of my childhood, wrapped as it is in many of my happiest memories. As it is for so many people, that room has always seemed to me the spiritual center of the home—the place that drew us all together with its aromas, its warmth, the magical way it produced delectable meals and unimaginable delights day after day.

It is with these sentiments in mind that we have created this kitchen companion. We hope it serves as a place for you to keep your favorite recipes, record your cooking secrets, organize your thoughts and time, and savor the wealth of experience that occurs somewhere between the crack of the first egg and the sinkful of dishes at the end of the meal.

RACHEL NEWMAN
EDITOR-IN-CHIEF
COUNTRY LIVING

DEDICATED TO
COUNTRY COOKS
—for your health,
happiness, and
fame as
good providers.

THE FARMER COUNTRY

KITCHEN COOK BOOK,

1894

Kitchen Notebook

_____

_____

_____

_____

_____

_____

_____

_____

_____

_____

_____

_____

_____

_____

_____

_____

**If you can organize
your kitchen,
you can organize
your life.**

LOUIS PARRISH

_____

_____

_____

_____

_____

_____

_____

_____

_____

_____

_____

_____

Empty dishes rattle loudly.

ANONYMOUS

_____

_____

_____

_____

_____

_____

_____

_____

FAVORITE RECIPES

Recipe _____

Book _____ Page _____

Recipe _____

Book _____ Page _____

Recipe _____

Book _____ Page _____

Recipe _____

Book _____ Page _____

Recipe _____

Book _____ Page _____

Recipe _____

Book _____ Page _____

Recipe _____

Book _____ Page _____

Recipe _____

Book _____ Page _____

Recipe _____

Book _____ Page _____

Recipe _____

Book _____ Page _____

Recipe _____

Book _____ Page _____

Recipe _____

Book _____ Page _____

Recipe _____

Book _____ Page _____

Recipe _____

Book _____ Page _____

Recipe _____

Book _____ Page _____

Recipe _____

Book _____ Page _____

Gifts from My Kitchen

cookies · bread · cranberry
bread · appl · · ueberry ja
· peach chutney · quince jelly · bre
and butter pickles · strawberry preserve
· herb butter · beach plum jelly
cranberry bread · applesauce · blueber
jam · jelly
bread · wber
preserve · a bre
· cran · · pesto
blueber · quin
jelly br · awber
pecan · read
cranber · lueber
jam · jelly
bread · wber
preserves · cookies · orange marmala
· cranberry bread · apple cider
quince jelly · bread and butter pick
· strawberry preserves · corn relish
garlic vinegar · blueberry jam · pea

Gift _____

To whom _____

Date / Occasion _____

Gift _____

To whom _____

Date / Occasion _____

Gift _____

To whom _____

Date / Occasion _____

Gift _____

To whom _____

Date / Occasion _____

Gift _____

To whom _____

Date / Occasion _____

Gift _____

To whom _____

Date / Occasion _____

Gift _____

To whom _____

Date / Occasion _____

Gift _____

To whom _____

Date / Occasion _____

Gift _____

To whom _____

Date / Occasion _____

Gift _____

To whom _____

Date / Occasion _____

Guide to Vinegars

Apple Cider: Strong flavor. All purpose.

Balsamic: Strong, robust flavor. All purpose,
but use sparingly.

Distilled White: Astringent flavor.
Good for mustards and creamy cheese dressings.

Herb: Mild to strong flavor. All purpose;
especially good for vinaigrettes.

Raspberry: Slightly sweet, fruity flavor.
Good for soups and vegetables. Mix with club soda
for a refreshing summer drink.

Wine: Pungent flavor. All purpose;
especially good for vinaigrettes.

Rice Wine: Mild, delicate flavor. Good for
sweet-and-sour dishes and marinated salads.

Sherry: Robust flavor.
Good for soups and stews.

Full o' beans
and benevolence!

ROBERT SMITH SURTEES

RESERVE FOR PRESERVES

Fruit	To make 1 quart preserves
Apples	2½ pounds
Apricots	2-2½ pounds
Blackberries	1½ quarts
Blueberries	1½ quarts
Cherries	2 pounds
Currants	1½ quarts
Peaches	2 pounds
Pears	2-2½ pounds
Plums	2 pounds
Quinces	2 pounds
Raspberries	1½ quarts
Rhubarb	2 pounds
Tomatoes	3 pounds

CANNING RECIPES

Economical people will seldom
use preserves, except for sickness.
They are unhealthy, expensive, and
useless to those who are well.

MRS. CHILD

The American Frugal Housewife, 1833

Party Recorder

If they like it,
it serves four;
otherwise, six.

ELSIE ZUSSMAN

DATE/OCCASION _____

GUESTS _____
_____
_____
_____
_____
_____

MENU _____
_____
_____
_____
_____

DATE/OCCASION _____

GUESTS _____
_____
_____
_____
_____
_____

MENU _____
_____
_____
_____
_____

DATE / OCCASION_____

GUESTS _____

_____

_____

_____

_____

MENU_____

_____

_____

_____

_____

DATE / OCCASION_____

GUESTS _____

_____

_____

_____

_____

MENU_____

_____

_____

_____

_____

Party Recorder

DATE/OCCASION_____

GUESTS _____
_____
_____
_____
_____

MENU_____
_____
_____
_____
_____

DATE/OCCASION_____

GUESTS _____
_____
_____
_____
_____

MENU_____
_____
_____
_____
_____

No bread.

Then bring me some toast!

PUNCH, 1852

B A K I N G   T I P S

Store all-purpose flour in a dry, dark, moderately cool place.
Store whole-wheat and
stone-ground flour in the refrigerator.

Check spices for freshness; if they are more than six months old,
you may have disappointing results. To keep track,
mark the containers with a purchase date.

Use a space at least 26 by 26 inches to roll out pastry
dough. Go just to the edge of the dough, but not over it;
this will keep the thickness even.

Try glass pie plates; they are sturdy, conduct heat evenly,
and allow you to see how the pastry is browning.

Cool most cakes in the pan on a rack 10 minutes. Then remove
the cake from the pan and let it cool right side up on a wire rack.

To prevent cakes from sticking to a wire cooling rack,
grease the rack lightly.

To even a cake-layer top, allow the cake to cool completely
on a rack. Replace it in the pan and using the rim as a guide,
run a long serrated knife across the top of the cake until
it is level with the rim.

COMMON
PAN SIZES

4 cups

1-quart baking dish or casserole
9- by $1\frac{1}{2}$-inch pie plate
8- by $1\frac{1}{2}$-inch round cake pan

6 cups

$1\frac{1}{2}$-quart baking dish or casserole
9- by $1\frac{1}{2}$-inch round cake pan
8- by 8- by $1\frac{1}{2}$-inch square pan
9- by 2-inch pie plate

8 cups

2-quart baking dish or casserole
8- by 8- by 2-inch square pan
9- by 5- by 3-inch loaf pan

COMMON CAN SIZES

6-ounce can . . . . ³⁄₄ cup
8-ounce can . . . . 1 cup
10½-ounce can . . . . 1¼ cups
12-ounce can . . . . 1½ cups
14-15½-ounce can . . . . 1¾ cups
1-pound can. . . . . 2 cups
1-pound 4-ounce can . . . . 2½ cups
1-pound 13-ounce can . . . . 3½ cups
3-pound 2-ounce can . . . . 5¾ cups

Simple Substitutions

Baking Powder . . . . 1 teaspoon = $\frac{1}{2}$ teaspoon
                                      cream of tartar plus
                                      $\frac{1}{4}$ teaspoon baking soda

Chocolate
(unsweetened) . . . . 1 ounce = 3 tablespoons
                                      unsweetened cocoa powder
                                      plus 1 tablespoon shortening

Cracker Crumbs . . . . . . $\frac{3}{4}$ cup = 1 cup dry
                                      bread crumbs

Cream (light) . . . . 1 cup = $\frac{7}{8}$ cup milk plus
                                      3 tablespoons butter

Cream (whipping) . . . . . . 1 cup = 2 cups whipped
                                      topping

Herbs . . . . 1 tablespoon finely cut
                                      fresh = 1 teaspoon dried

Milk (whole) . . . . 1 cup = $\frac{1}{2}$ cup evaporated
                                      milk plus $\frac{1}{2}$ cup water

Mustard (dry) . . . . 1 teaspoon = 1 tablespoon
                                      prepared mustard

Onion . . . . 1 small onion = 1 teaspoon
                                      onion powder

Sour Cream . . . . 1 cup = 1 cup plain yogurt

How much does it yield?

Apples: 1 medium . . . . 1 cup sliced

Beans (dry): 1 pound . . . . 2½ cups cooked

Bread: 1 slice (dry) . . . . ½ cup bread crumbs

Cornmeal: 1 cup . . . . 4 cups cooked

Dates: 1 pound . . . . 2½ cups pitted

Egg Whites: 7-10 . . . . 1 cup

Egg Yolks: 12-18 . . . . 1 cup

Fruit (dry): 1 pound . . . . 2⅔ cups cooked

Lemons: 1 medium . . . . ¼ cup juice

Oranges: 1 medium . . . . ⅓ cup juice

Pasta: 1 cup raw . . . . 2 cups cooked

Peanuts: 1 pound in the shell . . . . . . 2-2½ cups meats

Potatoes: 1 pound raw . . . . 2 cups mashed

Rice: 1 cup raw . . . . 3 cups cooked

Walnuts: 1 pound in the shell . . . . 2 cups meats

Cooking is like love.
It should be entered into with
abandon or not at all.

HARRIET VAN HORNE

GUIDE TO SEASONINGS

APPLES
Anise ✦ Cinnamon ✦ Cloves ✦ Ginger ✦ Nutmeg

BEEF STEW
Anise ✦ Bay leaf ✦ Mint ✦ Rosemary ✦ Sage

BEETS
Bay leaf ✦ Dill ✦ Tarragon ✦ Thyme

CABBAGE
Anise ✦ Caraway ✦ Oregano

CARROTS
Bay leaf ✦ Dill ✦ Marjoram ✦ Mint ✦ Tarragon ✦ Thyme

CHICKEN
Bay leaf ✦ Dill ✦ Marjoram ✦ Rosemary
Sage ✦ Tarragon ✦ Thyme

COLE SLAW
Caraway ✦ Celery seed ✦ Dill ✦ Mint ✦ Tarragon

CORNED BEEF
Bay leaf ✦ Dill ✦ Garlic ✦ Parsley

DUCK
Basil ✦ Oregano ✦ Sage ✦ Tarragon

LAMB
Chervil ✦ Marjoram ✦ Mint

MEAT LOAF
Cumin ✦ Nutmeg ✦ Oregano

PEARS
Cinnamon ✦ Coriander ✦ Ginger ✦ Mint

PEAS
Basil ✦ Marjoram ✦ Poppy seed ✦ Rosemary ✦ Savory

PORK
Caraway ✦ Marjoram ✦ Rosemary ✦ Sage

POT ROAST
Bay leaf ✦ Ginger ✦ Marjoram ✦ Thyme

POTATOES
Dill ✦ Parsley ✦ Rosemary

POTATO SALAD
Caraway ✦ Dill ✦ Oregano ✦ Parsley ✦ Sesame Seed

RICE
Basil ✦ Cinnamon ✦ Dill ✦ Parsley ✦ Saffron

SUMMER SQUASH
Basil ✦ Garlic ✦ Mace

SWEET POTATOES
Cinnamon ✦ Ginger ✦ Mace ✦ Nutmeg

TOMATO SALAD
Basil ✦ Dill ✦ Parsley ✦ Tarragon ✦ Thyme

TURNIPS
Caraway ✦ Dill ✦ Rosemary

WINTER SQUASH
Cinnamon ✦ Clove ✦ Dill ✦ Mace

Guide to Common Apples

Cortland: Red and green skin with white flesh; crisp and juicy. Good for snacks and for pies and baking.

Golden Russet: Gold skin with tart flesh. Good for eating raw and for cider.

Granny Smith: Bright, shiny green skin with greenish, juicy flesh. All purpose.

Jonathan: Bright red skin with hard, tart flesh. All purpose.

Macoun: Deep-red skin with crisp, tart flesh. Good for eating raw and for cakes and pies.

McIntosh: Red skin with aromatic flesh. Good for eating raw, for juicy pies, and for applesauce.

Northern Spy: Red and green skin with hard, juicy flesh. All purpose.

Red Delicious: Dark red striped or blushed skin with hard yellowish flesh; sweet. Good for eating raw and for Waldorf salad.

Spartan: Bright red skin with juicy flesh. Good for eating raw and for salads.

Winesap: Deep red skin with hard, tart flesh. Good for pies and for baking whole.

Yellow Delicious: Gold skin and flesh. Good for all baking, for eating raw, and for cakes and pies.

I know the look of an apple
that is roasting and sizzling on a
hearth on a winter's evening, and I
know the comfort that comes
of eating it hot, along with some
sugar and a drench of cream.

MARK TWAIN

Holiday Organizer

MENUS

_____

_____

_____

_____

_____

_____

_____

_____

_____

_____

_____

_____

_____

_____

_____

_____

_____

_____

_____

_____

_____

_____

MENUS

_____

_____

_____

_____

_____

_____

_____

_____

_____

_____

_____

_____

_____

_____

_____

_____

_____

_____

_____

_____

_____

_____

_____

_____

_____

_____

_____

_____

_____

RECIPES

RECIPES

_____

_____

_____

_____

_____

_____

_____

_____

_____

_____

_____

_____

_____

_____

_____

_____

_____

_____

_____

_____

_____

_____

_____

_____

_____

Planning Ahead

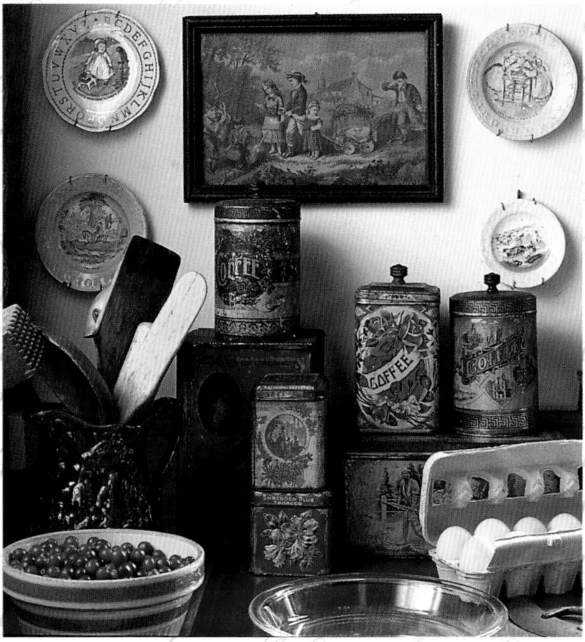

5 DAYS AHEAD _____

_____

_____

_____

_____

_____

_____

_____

4 DAYS AHEAD _____

_____

_____

_____

_____

_____

_____

3 DAYS AHEAD _____

_____

_____

_____

_____

_____

_____

_____

2 DAYS AHEAD

_____

_____

_____

_____

_____

_____

_____

_____

1 DAY AHEAD

_____

_____

_____

_____

_____

_____

_____

SAME DAY

_____

_____

_____

_____

_____

_____

_____

_____

Roasting Timetable

	Temperature	Minutes per pound
BEEF		
Tenderloin	425° F	10-15
Top Round Roast		
Rare	325° F	23
Medium	325° F	23-25
CHICKEN	350° F	25
DUCKLING	350° F	30-35
GOOSE		
Unstuffed	350° F	16
Stuffed	350° F	20
HAM (processed)		
Half Ham	325° F	30
Whole Ham	325° F	25
LAMB		
Crown Roast		
Rare	325° F	15-20
Medium	325° F	25-30
Well Done	325° F	30-35
Leg		
Rare	325° F	20-25
Medium	325° F	25-30
Well Done	325° F	30-35
TURKEY		
Unstuffed	350° F	20
Stuffed	350° F	25

Progress in civilization
has been accompanied by
progress in cookery.

FANNIE FARMER

All happiness depends on a leisurely breakfast.

JOHN GUNTHER

_____

_____

_____

_____

_____

_____

_____

_____

_____

_____

_____

_____

Better to be neat and tidy
than tight and needy.

PROVERB

_____

_____

_____

_____

_____

_____

_____

_____

_____

What I say is
that, if a man
really likes
potatoes,
he must be a
pretty decent
sort of fellow.

A . A .   M I L N E

A lmost every person has
something secret he likes to eat.

M.F.K. FISHER

Soup of the evening,
beau—ootiful soo—oop!

LEWIS CARROLL

REFRIGERATOR STORAGE

Fresh Fruit

Apples. . . . . 1 month

Bananas, Melons, Nectarines,
  Peaches, Pears, Plums . . . . 5 days

Berries, Cherries. . . . . 3 days

Citrus Fruit. . . . . 2 weeks

Fresh Vegetables

Beets, Carrots, Parsnips,
  Radishes, Turnips . . . . 2 weeks

Broccoli . . . . 5 days

Cabbage, Cauliflower, Cucumber, Eggplant,
  Green Beans, Onions, Peppers . . . . . . 1 week

Corn. . . . . 1 day

Leafy Greens . . . . 5 days

Lima Beans, Peas. . . . . 2 days

Tomatoes. 1 week

Dairy Products

Butter . . . . 2-3 weeks

Buttermilk, Sour Cream, Yogurt. . 2 weeks

Cheese (slices). . . . . 2 weeks

       (whole pieces). . . . . 1 month

Cottage Cheese, Ricotta. . . . . 5 days

Cream. . . . . 1 week

Eggs (in shell). . . . . 1 month

     (whites, yolks). . . . . 4 days

Margarine. 1 month

Milk. . . . . 1 week

Meat, Fish and Poultry
Fresh Meat (beef, lamb, pork, veal)
Chops, Steaks . . . . .3 days
Ground Meat, Stew Meat . . . . 2 days
Roasts . . . . 3 days
Sausage (fresh) . . . . 2 days
Variety Meats . . . . .2 days

Processed Meats
Bacon, Frankfurters . . . . 2 weeks
Ham
   canned (unopened) . . . . 6 months
   slices . . . . .3 days
   whole . . . . .1 week
Sausage (dry) . . . . 3 weeks
Luncheon Meats . . . . 5 days

Fish, Shellfish (all kinds)
Fresh or thawed. . . . . 1 day

Poultry (all kinds)
Fresh or thawed . . . . 2 days

Cooked or Canned Foods
Broths, Gravies, Soups . . . . 2 days
Casseroles, Stews. . . . . 3 days
Fruit, Vegetables. . . . . 3 days
Juices, Drinks. . . . . 6 days
Meat, Fish, Poultry. . . . . 2 days
Stuffings. .2 days

KITCHEN EQUIVALENTS

Temperatures

°F (FAHRENHEIT)   °C (CENTIGRADE)

203 (water simmers) 95

212 (water boils) 100

225 (very slow oven) 107.2

300 (slow oven) 149

350 (moderate oven) 177

375 (moderate oven) 191

400 (hot oven) 205

425 218

450 232

500 (very hot oven) 260

Measures

3 teaspoons . . . . .1 tablespoon

8 tablespoons . . . . .½ cup

16 tablespoons . . . . .1 cup

1 liquid ounce . . . . .2 tablespoons

4 liquid ounces . . . . .½ cup

2 cups . . . . 1 pint

4 cups . . . . 1 quart

4 quarts . . . . 1 gallon

1 pound . . . . 16 ounces

Units of Weight

$\frac{1}{4}$ ounce . . . . 7 grams

$\frac{1}{3}$ ounce . . . . 10 grams

$\frac{1}{2}$ ounce . . . . 14 grams

1 ounce . . . . 28 grams

$1\frac{3}{4}$ ounces . . . . .50 grams

4 ounces ($\frac{1}{4}$ pound) . . . . .114 grams

8 ounces ($\frac{1}{2}$ pound) . . . . 227 grams

1.1 pounds . . . . 500 grams

2.2 pounds . . . . 1,000 grams (1 kilogram)

Liquid Measures

U.S. SPOONS &   METRIC EQUIVALENTS
CUPS

1 teaspoon. . . . . 5 milliliters

1 tablespoon . . . . .15 milliliters

$3\frac{1}{3}$ tablepoons. . . . .$\frac{1}{2}$ deciliter
(50 milliliters)

$\frac{1}{4}$ cup . . . . 60 milliliters

$\frac{1}{3}$ cup . . . . 85 milliliters

$\frac{1}{3}$ cup plus 1 tablespoon . . . . .1 deciliter
(100 milliliters)

1 cup . . . . .240 milliliters

1 cup plus $1\frac{1}{4}$ tablespoons . . . . . $\frac{1}{4}$ liter

2 cups plus $2\frac{1}{2}$ tablespoons . . . . .$\frac{1}{2}$ liter

4 cups . . . . 960 milliliters

$4\frac{1}{3}$ cups . . . . 1 liter
(1,000 milliliters)

FREQUENT
PHONE NUMBERS

Name_____

Phone number_____

Name_____

Phone number_____

Name_____

Phone number_____

Name_____

Phone number_____

Name_____

Phone number_____

Name_____

Phone number_____

Name_____

Phone number_____

Name _____

Phone number _____

Name _____

Phone number _____

Name _____

Phone number _____

Name _____

Phone number _____

Name _____

Phone number _____

Name _____

Phone number _____

Name _____

Phone number _____

Name _____

Phone number _____

Name _____

Phone number _____

Name _____

Phone number _____

Name _____

Phone number _____

Name _____

Phone number _____

Name _____

Phone number _____

Name _____

Phone number _____

Name _____

Phone number _____

Name _____

Phone number _____

Name _____

Phone number _____

Name _____

Phone number _____

CREDITS & ACKNOWLEDGMENTS

Slipcase Photograph by Jon Elliott. **1** Photograph by Jessie Walker and Arthur Griggs. **3** Photograph by Jon Elliott. **6** Photograph by Paul Kopelow. **8** Excerpt from *The Farmer Country Kitchen Cook Book*, 1894, reprinted by The Webb Company, 1973; photograph by Keith Scott Morton. **10** Excerpt from *Cooking as Therapy* by Louis Parrish. **11** Photograph by Paul Kopelow. **12** Photograph by Keith Scott Morton. **13** Photograph by Keith Scott Morton. **15** Photograph by Jeremy Samuelson. **16** Photograph by Jeff McNamara. **17** Photograph by Keith Scott Morton. **20** Photograph by Jessie Walker. **22** Photograph by Jessie Walker. **23** Photograph by Jerry Simpson. **25** Photograph by Doug Kennedy. **26** Excerpt from *Farmer's Almanac and House Keeper's Receipt Book* for 1851. Reprinted in *America and Her Almanacs* by Robb Sagendorph, 1970; photograph by Keith Scott Morton.
28 Excerpt from *Handley Cross* by Robert Smith Surtees. **29** Photograph by Jessie Walker. **33** Excerpt from *The American Frugal Housewife* by Mrs.Child, 1833. **34** Photograph by Keith Scott Morton. **35** Excerpt from "On Making Chicken Soup" by Elsie Zussman, *The New York Times*, April 1, 1974. **36** Photograph by Paul Kopelow. **37** Photograph by Keith Scott Morton. **40** Photograph by Jessie Walker. **42** Excerpt from *Punch*, vol. xxii, 1852. **43** Photograph by Jessie Walker. **45** Photograph by Jessie Walker. **46** Photograph by Keith Scott Morton. **47** Photograph by Keith Scott Morton. **48** Photograph by Paul Kopelow. **52** Excerpt by Harriet Van Horne from *Vogue,* October 1956. **53** Photograph by Keith Scott Morton. **56** Photograph by Keith Scott Morton. **57** Photograph by Keith Scott Morton. **58** Photograph by Keith Scott Morton. **60** Excerpt from *Mark Twain's Autobiography* by Mark Twain, 1924. **61** Photograph by Paul Kopelow. **62** Photograph by Jeremy Samuelson. **64** Photograph by Keith Scott Morton. **67** Photograph by Kari Haavisto. **70** Photograph by Keith Scott Morton. **71** Photograph by Keith Scott Morton. **74** Excerpt from *The Boston Cooking-School Cook Book* by Fannie Farmer, 1896; photograph by Keith Scott Morton. **76** Photograph by Keith Scott Morton. **77** Excerpt by John Gunther from *Newsweek*, April 14, 1959. **79** Photograph by Jeremy Samuelson. **80** Photograph by Keith Scott Morton. **81** Photograph by Keith Scott Morton. **82** Excerpt from *Not That It Matters* by A. A. Milne; photograph by Keith Scott Morton. **85** Photograph by Keith Scott Morton. **86** Excerpt from *Alice in Wonderland* by Lewis Carroll, 1865; photograph by Paul Kopelow. **92** Photograph by Keith Scott Morton.